BIBLE STORIES

Illustrated Stories from the Old Testament

BIBLE STORIES

Illustrated Stories from the Old Testament

ILLUSTRATIONS BY **MANUELA ADREANI**

TEXT EDITED BY **FEDERICA MAGRIN**

WSkids
WHITE STAR KIDS

CONTENTS

INTRODUCTION

The Bible is the most widely read book in the world; indeed, for very many people, it is also the most important because it contains the teachings and the word of God, transcribed and collected by a variety of authors, at different times, in multiple languages, and assembled into many different books.

Did you know the word "bible" means "books" in ancient Greek? There are seventy-three books in the Bible, forty-six of which form the Old Testament and recount events between the creation of the world and the birth of Jesus. They describe the Hebrew people, their ancestors, their kings and the prophets who shaped history.

Some very remarkable individuals come to life in these ancient texts!

The pages you are about to read present the most famous events described in the Bible. You'll meet Adam and Eve, Noah, Abraham, Moses, Joseph and other protagonists of the Old Testament.

You'll find their stories are full of lessons and advice, not to mention incredible adventures, promises broken and kept, mistakes, repentance and forgiveness, and essentially, faith and love.

CREATION

Before the sky and land existed, chaos reigned on Earth. The world was a bleak, inhospitable place in which life was not possible. There were none of the great and extraordinary things we have around us today, like mountains, seas, plains and forests, and there was not a single, tiny creature in this dark and desolate land.

Prompted by a rush of boundless love, God began to create everything in the universe. He wanted the world to be perfect and it took him seven days to complete his work. This first thing he did was divide the water into two separate places, the water under and the water over, a primordial ocean of sorts, but with neither fish nor alga in it. It was a dark place in which chaos still reigned and no form of life, even the most basic, could survive.

It was for this reason that God decided there should be light – warm, powerful rays that would allow the future inhabitants of the world to thrive and multiply, without fear of the impenetrable darkness. The dark hours remained only at night, a time assigned to rest, in memory of the shadows and fear of old, and antithesis to the new light and hope.

After the first day, God divided the sky from the land, and named the canopy he created the firmament.

He placed it up high so that it could be admired and make people dream when looking up at if from far below.

As the second day came to an end, God continued in his work, gathering together the water to form oceans, seas, lakes, rivers, streams and swamps. On the dry ground, which was occasionally wetted by water which fell as rain, he grew every kind of plant, creating enormous plains and forests to provide wood and shade. Some species of vegetation were made to bear fruit and seeds, so that they might multiply and grow dense.

The world was a much more welcoming place than before – the ideal environment for more complex life forms to develop.

On the fourth day, God added two great "lamps" to the things he had created so far: one big, bright one, the Sun, to provide light and warmth during the day; and another smaller, fainter one, the Moon, to brighten the nocturnal hours.

Creation was now ready to host living creatures.

And so on the fifth day, God commanded the seas, oceans, rivers and lakes to be filled with fish and other animals able to live underwater, like jellyfish, dolphins, whales; he bid the sky be populated with birds, small ones like hummingbirds, and also giant ones like pelicans, and all other winged animals that were able to fly.

Earth became an incredibly populated place. Creatures of unimaginable shapes and startling colors swam in its waters, with fins to move quickly and gills to breath, while the blue sky was invaded by chirping flocks of every kind of bird, some who beat their wings to move from place to place, others who soared on the wind. God was enchanted by his work and asked the sea creatures and the winged creatures to multiply and populate all corners of the planet, even the most remote that seemed impossible to reach.

His creation was truly wonderful and worthy of admiration, but God was still not satisfied. He felt something important was missing and so, on the sixth day, he ordered the ground to be occupied by a profusion of animal species – cattle, like goats, oxen and sheep, which were easy to tame; wild beasts, like lions, elephants and bears, which were wild and difficult to approach; and reptiles, from tiny lizards to great snakes, destined to forever crawl on the ground, eating dust lifted by their bodies.

Everything he had created so far was great and deserving of praise, but God still felt something was missing, so did his best to make sure the world would be perfect by the time he finished. He ordered a living creature to be brought forth in his image, and in his own image he created people; he created them male and female, different but equally important, so that when they came together, they could have children and populate the earth.

To man and woman, God gave another important job, that of looking after the animals and plants, tending them with love. From the land, they would have everything they needed to survive and proliferate, together with their children and their children's children, for many generations; they had herbs and seeds to feed on, others to feed to the cattle. They had everything they needed to eat and clothe themselves.

At the end of the sixth day, God looked at all that he had made and was supremely happy: above him was the firmament, with the Sun, the Moon and the stars to illuminate and show the way; below was the land, covered by water, forests, plains and deserts, where animals and mankind could live in peace. What he saw was the perfect reflection of his plan and a tangible sign of his immense love for the whole of creation.

On the seventh day, having completed his work, God decided to rest, to allow himself time to admire what he had created, in both the Sky and on Land. He did nothing the whole day but observe the incredible sight before his eyes, the marvel of the trees, the flowers, the animals and mankind, and from that moment, he decided the seventh day would be forever devoted to rest and reflection on how beautiful and unique Earth was.

This was how everything around us was created – the Universe, Earth and Living Creatures.

ADAM AND EVE

The story of the first people dates to time immemorial, when the Earth itself had just been created. It was back then that God decided to take a handful of dust from the ground and make it into the shape of a man – a mere puppet that started to breathe and to move only when God breathed the breath of life into his nostrils.

For a home, God gave man the Garden of Eden, a place located eastward in which every kind of plant grew and assured the new visitor a bounteous supply of fruit. In the middle of the garden was a special tree, the tree of life, which gave knowledge of good and evil. When God showed the man the many wonders of the garden, he stated clearly that it was forbidden to eat the fruit of this tree.

And so the man began his life in this enchanted place, eating the plants and fruit that grew there and living a life without toil or labor.

Very soon, the man began to feel lonely, so God decided to surround him with animals of all kinds.

One by one, he brought before the man the many creatures populating the skies, the land and the water, and asked him to give them a name. The man named them all but despite being surrounded by a multitude of different species, he still felt he hadn't found the companion he sought.

God realized that what the man needed was someone similar with whom to speak and share his day. He caused a deep sleep to fall on the man so that he could remove one of his ribs and, with it, create woman.

On reawakening, the man wondered at the beauty of the new creature moulded from his own body and therefore a part of him. God ordered that they be considered husband and wife from that moment and that their union last in eternity. For some time, the couple lived happily in the garden, where they walked naked without feeling shame and had no worries of any kind.

The woman encountered a serpent one day and it asked her, "I heard you humans cannot eat the fruit of the tree of life. Is this true?"

The woman replied, "We can take any fruit we wish, but not from the tree in the center of the garden. If we do, we will die right away."

The serpent replied that this was not true, and they would never risk death by eating only one piece of fruit. "If anything," he continued, persuasively, "you will be like God and know everything if you do."

The woman went to look closer and noticed for the first time that the fruit on the tree of life was more enticing than all the others. She thought for a long time about what the serpent had said and was unable to resist. She picked a fruit and took it to her husband.

They ate it together whereupon they became aware of their nakedness. The fruit had given them knowledge of good and evil they had not had before, and it made them sew fig leaves together to cover themselves.

Moments later, on hearing God approach, the man ran to hide behind a plant.

"Why did you run away?" God asked when he saw the man hiding.

"Because I am ashamed that I am naked."

Surprised at the man's reply, God asked, "How do you know you are naked?" then continued, "Have you eaten from the tree of life?"

The man nodded, and God asked why he had done it.

"My wife brought the fruit to me and I succumbed to the temptation to taste it."

God turned to the woman, "Why did you do this when I told you it was forbidden?"

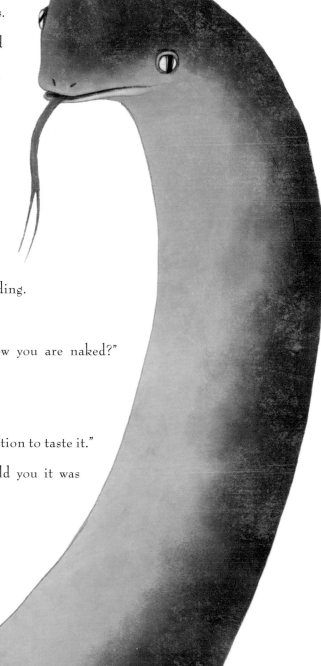

The woman told of how she had met the serpent and it had deceived her, telling her that nothing serious would happen if she ate from the tree of life.

God became angry and cursed the serpent. "For what you have done, you and all your descendants shall be condemned to crawl on the ground and eat dust.

Between you and the woman there shall be no friendship, only hatred.

You will try to bite her heel and she will crush you with her foot."

God's anger then turned on the man and woman, to whom he announced they would now have to toil to obtain from the ground the things they had previously picked without effort. After imposing their punishment, God ordered both man and woman to leave the wonders of Eden and to live forever in hostile lands.

When they were forced to abandon their earthly paradise, the man took the name Adam and he named his wife Eve, because she would be the mother of all men.

From their union, two very different children were born, Cain and Abel. Growing up, Cain wanted to be a farmer and Abel a shepherd. When the boys had become men, they decided to offer up to God part of their daily produce one day. Cain gathered the most succulent fruit while Abel sacrificed a few of his sheep. God favored Abel's sacrifice more, and Cain lost his temper with both the Lord and his brother. His anger mounted until he could endure it no longer and one merciless day, he murdered Abel.

When God learned what Cain had done, he drove him from the land and banished him to a life without peace, wandering from place to place. He would also have to work much harder than before to reap even the smallest of fruits from the land.

Cain accepted his fate and settled in Nod, opposite Eden. He met a woman, they married, and she gave birth to a child, Enoch, who built a city and became the head of a large family.

Adam and Eve also had another child, named Set. He brought new joy to the couple after they lost their first two children, one murdered, the other sent away.

NOAH'S ARK

For a long time, the world was an enchanted place in which animals and man lived together in peace. Bubbles burst forth from the silver waters of rivers while brightly-colored fish leapt through them; the cold depths of lakes provided a home to creatures of every type; and the powerful waves of the sea hid animals of the most wonderful shapes and sizes. The forests were leafy and dense, the mountains lined with shrubs and vegetation, the mountaintops coated with snow all year around, while the verdant plains were crossed by herds of grazing animals, predators following on their heels. Birds circled the skies while the animals had learned to live together in the deserts, forests and prairies. There was food enough for everyone and harmony reigned supreme.

But this joyful time was soon replaced by a much sadder one.

Men and women had become greedy and arrogant, they had forgotten the beauty of the natural world around them and how they should thank God for it all. War, corruption and enmity had replaced peace, justice and kindness. Even animals could no longer find a peaceful way of living together. The whole of creation was once again in the grip of chaos.

God waited and watched, hoping humanity would repent and return to obeying his laws, but the day came when he realized nothing could restore his kingdom to its former glory. Bitterly disappointed, he decided he would have to start afresh, like an artist rejecting a painting and reaching out for a blank new canvas. The only way to achieve it was a flood that would sweep away all that was wicked and allow the few remaining good things to flourish once more.

For this task, God chose Noah. Unlike other men, Noah had continued to behave as God required, looking after his family, tending to the animals in his care, and honoring God every day.

"Noah," God said, "it is with a heavy heart that I have decided to send a great storm that will flood the world and wipe out wickedness forthwith. I don't want anything to happen to you or

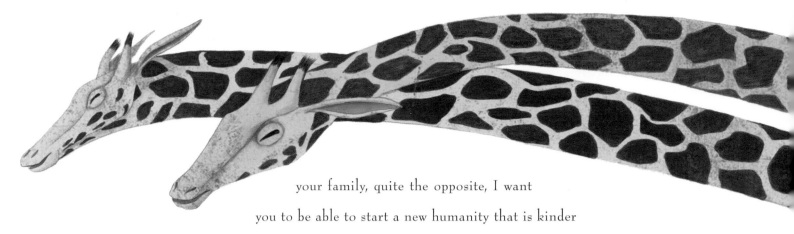

your family, quite the opposite, I want

you to be able to start a new humanity that is kinder

and more just. For this reason, I ask you to build an ark, an enormous vessel that is big enough to hold seven pairs of clean animals and two pairs of unclean animals. Use strong wood and daub it inside and out with pitch to make it watertight. You must also build a roof on top to stop the rain from entering. I will warn you when the time comes, so you can bring inside the animals, your family and enough food for all."

Noah was shocked at what he heard but did exactly as God commanded, sawing planks of sturdy wood and joining them together to build the ark. When the great vessel was complete, he daubed it with tar and filled it with food.

God returned to Noah and announced that the floods would soon come. "In seven days, I will make the rains start and they will last forty days and forty nights. Prepare everything before that day comes, as I have advised, and you will be safe."

Noah, who was six hundred years old at the time, again did as he was instructed. He herded the many species of animals inside the ark then asked his wife, their three children, Sem, Cam and Iafet, and their wives, to take refuge onboard.

The seventh day came, the sky filled with dark clouds, and outside it became as black as night.

The Sun disappeared, and in its place, a blanket of darkness fell over Earth. Seconds later, torrential rain began to crash down, cold and fierce, beating on the trees and houses. Water engulfed the plains and forests, and the oceans grew so big and violent they broke their banks and flooded the deserts and hills. As time went on, Earth vanished from sight. Even the highest mountaintop disappeared under a sheet of black, angry water.

The Ark floated on the surface, at the mercy of the heaving waters, and looking out of the tiny window at the top, Noah couldn't see anything bar the storm that raged on.

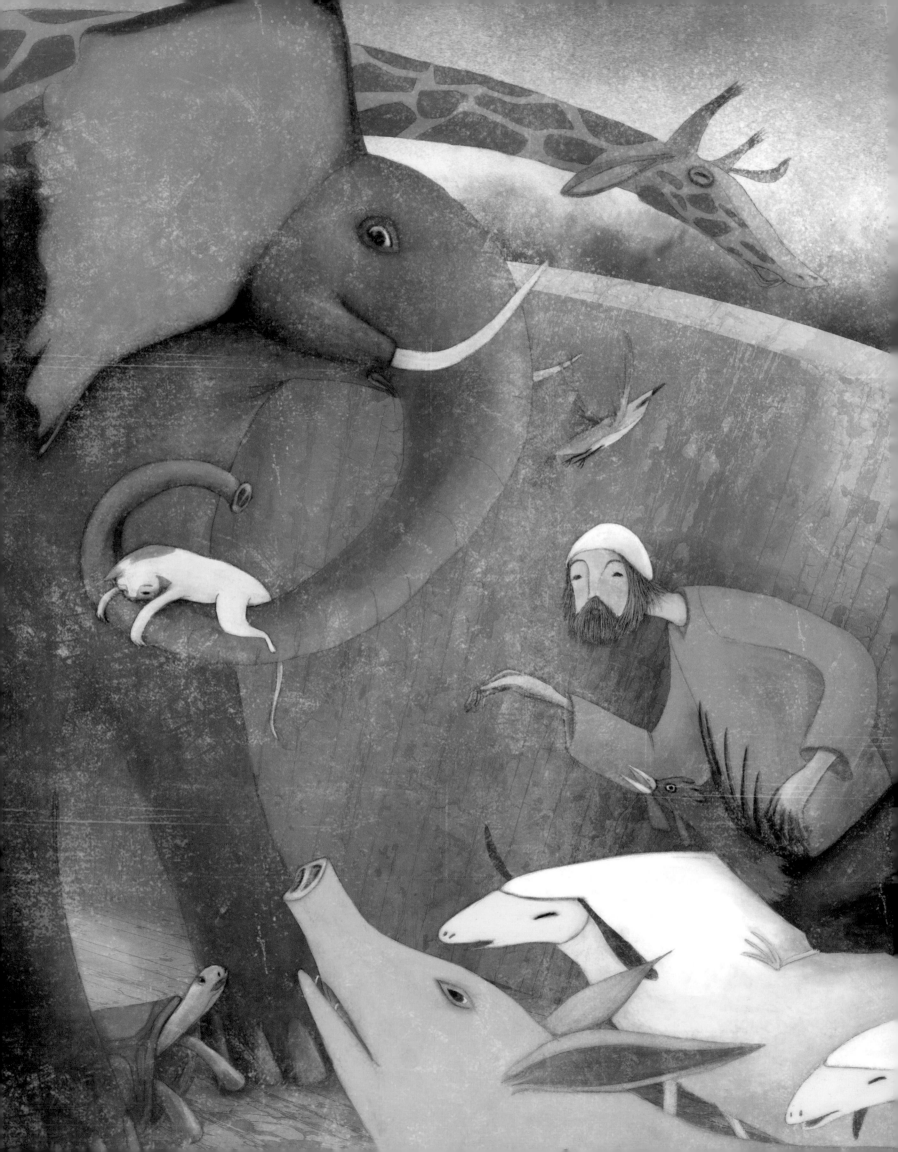

It remained thus for forty days and forty nights. Inside the Ark, Noah, his family and all their animals were safe, they ate the food they had packed and waited for the storm to end with hope in their hearts.

A howling wind whipped up from nowhere, the gusts so violent they swept away the clouds and dried up some of the water. In the seventh month after the flood, the ark carrying Noah and the animals came to rest atop Mount Ararat, and after another three months, mountaintops began to reappear around them.

The world still seemed under water, so Noah sent out a raven then a dove to find somewhere to build a new home. Both returned, having found no trace of dry land.

The flood had been so mighty, they had to wait several more days before the water receded enough. When Noah finally sent the dove out again in search of a sign, it returned with an olive branch in its beak. Noah could hardly contain his joy – Earth was flourishing once again, and producing trees and flowers. God had kept his promise and they were safe!

"Noah," God called him, "you and your family can now leave the ark. The world has returned to what it once was, and it will be home to you and all the animals you have brought with you, now and for generations in the future. You have my blessing and I promise to never again send such a mighty flood. As a sign of this covenant, a bow of many colors will form in the sky to remember the bond between the sky and the land." As God spoke, an enormous rainbow appeared in the sky. "All those who see it will remember this promise and God's love for all creatures who laud him with a good and righteous life."

Noah became a farmer. He would occasionally raise his eyes to the sky as he happily tended his vines, seeking out the rainbow that would remind him of God's promise - to him, his children and to the new world he'd created.

THE TOWER OF BABEL

People were not always divided into nations, their lands were not always divided by borders, and men could once speak easily to one another, having just one language that they all understood. As a result, people who lived in the north were equal to those who lived in the south, and those who had decided to settle in the east resembled those who had set up home in the west. People lived together in peace and came together regularly to celebrate the extraordinary world that God had given them.

There came a day, however, when some men settled in a land called Shinar, in the far east, and built a city that was bigger and more spectacular than any other. They wanted to rival nature and create something that would equal the magnificence of the mountains, forests and oceans.

Such a construction had never been attempted before, and to build this one, the people baked an endless supply of bricks in enormous kilns. Bricks would be much stronger than the stone normally used, and by bonding the bricks with tar, they would withstand the weather much better than simple mortar.

They agreed to erect an enormous tower in the center of the city, one so high it would reach the sky, and so grand anyone seeing it would gaze in amazement. Anyone looking up at it from below would not be able to see the top, which would reach into the clouds.

The construction of the houses and public buildings in the city required considerable effort. Craftsmen and laborers, led by architects and engineers, worked day and night, year after year, to complete the many buildings, but erecting the tower was an even more gruelling task.

The people looked on with pride as the building of the tower progressed, floor after floor.

"It's the most beautiful thing ever created!" someone exclaimed.

"Nothing in nature can compare to the tower!" someone else applauded.

"Now that we have the tower, we need a name that sets us apart from the rest of the world," someone suggested.

"Yes," someone else replied. "We're not like anyone else. We have built this city and this magnificent tower!"

"Right," yet someone else echoed. "We are different. We are better because we have built something unique and unsurpassable."

Their clamor reached the ears of God, who was always listening and watching over Creation. He was deeply wounded at what he heard as he had created mankind to live in harmony with each other, no one person superior or inferior to another, and sharing the world with animals. He had not created man from dust so that he might challenge God and try to take his place!

He was disappointed with the people who had erected the tower and those who had praised it, but God realized it was in man's nature to want to excel and rival God. He did not strike the tower down with a bolt of lightning nor did he send a messenger to bring humanity to its senses; what he did was cause the people, from that day, to divide into different lands and to have different characteristics, immediately speaking a different way. The city was abandoned and the grand tower it hosted become known as the Tower of Babel, meaning "confused and chaotic place." Indeed, it was after its construction that people started to speak different languages, making communication between peoples almost impossible.

ABRAHAM AND ISAAC

What would you do if you were told to leave your house and seek a new home in a distant land you had never heard of? Very few people, would give up their home to settle somewhere unknown. But not Abraham. He was a very special man who lived until he was one hundred years old and filled the world with children and the promise of hope for the future. When God asked him to leave for the Promised Land, taking with him his wife Sara and his few belongings, Abraham, a righteous man of unwavering faith, did as he was instructed and set off for Canaan where he built a new home.

Even though the arduous journey through unknown territories had been an ample test of Abraham's faith, God tested it again a few years later. He and Sarah were very advanced in age by then and had given up all hope of having a child, but God announced that Sarah would bear a son, the first of a long line of descendants for Abraham.

The couple could hardly believe it to begin with. How could it be possible, at Sarah's age? But despite the absurdity of it, Abraham and his wife believed the happy announcement of her pregnancy and were rewarded nine months later with the birth of a healthy, robust baby they called Isaac.

A few years later, when Isaac had grown enough to accompany his father in his work, Abraham received another request from God. "I am about to ask a great sacrifice of you," God said. "You must give me your son, Isaac, as proof of your love."

Abraham was deeply distressed by the demand. Why would God want him to conceive a child only to take him away so soon?

Despite being distraught at the request, Abraham reluctantly agreed. With deep sadness in his heart, he prepared wood for the altar and asked Isaac to accompany him to the mountain for a sacrifice to God.

Upon reaching the mountaintop, Abraham made to carry out God's request, but a celestial messenger stopped him. "Don't do it!" the angel called out, placing a hand on Abraham's arm. "God now knows the depth of your love. He knows you would have sacrificed your son to prove your faith. In truth, God never intended you to actually do it, he wanted to know how far you would go to carry out his will."

Abraham rejoiced at God's decision and loved him even more for the kindness shown in saving the life of his beloved son Isaac.

At that moment, Abraham saw a great ram in the thicket, caught by its horns, and sacrificed the animal instead of his son. With tears of joy in his eyes, he lauded God for his benevolence.

JOSEPH AND
HIS BROTHERS

Jacob had many children and although he loved them all like only a father can, he had a genuine preference for the youngest, because he had been born to him in his old age when he thought he would have no more children. From birth, Joseph had held a special place in his father's heart which was why Jacob directed most of his attentions to him and lavished precious gifts upon him.

The elder brothers were jealous, even more so when Joseph began to have premonitory dreams in which it became clear his life would be special and they would all have to bow before him.

Jacob asked Joseph one day to check if all was going well with his brothers, who had taken the sheep to graze near Shechem. To please his father, whom he loved dearly, the young Joseph set off to reach his brothers. When they saw him arrive, they plotted to kill him. Luckily, they changed their minds at the last minute and sold him to a trader headed to Egypt instead.

So, for twenty shekels of silver, Joseph was taken as a slave to the distant land of Egypt while his brothers returned home to tell their father that his beloved youngest son had been torn apart by a wild beast.

While Jacob wept in Canaan for his son's death, Joseph found himself serving in the household of Potiphar, a very powerful man and captain of the Pharaoh's guard. Within no time, Joseph proved to his master that he could administer with skill the many things entrusted to him. As a result, Potiphar gave Joseph charge of the palace. Unfortunately, Potiphar's wife also laid eyes on Joseph and became enamored of him. Feeling a duty of respect towards the man who had taken him under his wing, Joseph refused the woman. He could never have imagined she would

seek revenge and cause him to be arrested and imprisoned.

Joseph was not only his father's favourite, he was also very much loved by God, who has been secretly watching over him since his birth. It was with God's divine intervention that the prison warden recognized Joseph's talents and gave him an important role in the running of the prison.

During his imprisonment, Joseph was often summoned to interpret dreams. It was a gift he had always possessed, and which set him apart from everyone else.

This same skill brought him not long after before the Pharaoh. The Egyptian king had had two nightmares which worried him a great deal. In fact, he felt they had been sent to warn him about something, but he couldn't make any sense of them.

The royal cupbearer advised the Pharaoh to summon Joseph who had once helped him interpret a dream. Joseph was called before the king.

"I can find no peace," the Pharaoh said. "A few nights ago, I dreamt of seven fat cows and then seven lean cows, and then seven good ears of corn which dried up before my eyes. I know it must mean something, but I don't know what…"

"The seven fat cows, like the seven good ears of corn, are seven years of plenty," Joseph explained, "whereas the seven lean cows and seven dry ears of corn are seven years of hunger. You must gather enough wheat in the years of plenty so that you will not suffer when the ground becomes arid and produces no fruit in the years of hunger."

The Pharaoh was deeply troubled by what Joseph said. If what the man had foretold was correct, he would have to be extremely careful or his kingdom could end up without food in the drought years. Despite his initial puzzlement, the king believed Joseph's interpretation and decided to appoint him administrator of the kingdom, giving him his ring to signal they would be equals in governing decisions.

And so the former slave and prisoner was given the task of managing the country's resources and assure its prosperity.

As foretold, for seven years abundant rain fell, rendering the fields fertile and producing wheat that exceeded their expectations. Now viceroy, Joseph ordered all surpluses to be kept in the storehouses. After seven years of abundance, when water no longer fell on the desert plains and the plants began to wither, the storehouses were opened to feed the people and animals.

Now, you should know that the drought affected not only the area around the river Nile, but also vast neighboring areas, including Canaan. Jacob sent his sons to Egypt with enough money to buy grain for their family and their animals.

After many years, the brothers found themselves face-to-face with Joseph.

As you can imagine, they didn't recognize him and believing him to be a man of importance, bowed before him. Joseph had no trouble remembering his brothers or what they had done to him. For this reason, he wished to accuse them of being spies and have the guards throw them out. But he thought twice about it and decided to seek an agreement with them instead. He would give them wheat if they returned with their younger brother, the son born to Jacob and Joseph's mother after Joseph had gone away to Egypt. News that he had a younger brother had moved him deeply and he desperately wanted to meet him!

Joseph's brothers, laden with wheat given to them by a man they believed the viceroy of Egypt, returned to their father and told him of the governor's request.

For a long time, Jacob refused to send his youngest son Benjamin to a distant, foreign land. He feared he might lose him as had happened with his beloved Joseph.

The time came, though, when their food stores began to run so low he had to relent.

The brothers, Benjamin included, set off on foot for Egypt to meet the viceroy again.

Joseph welcomed them enthusiastically. Even though his brothers had been very cruel to him, he couldn't help but love them dearly.

Unaware they were before their brother, Jacob's sons were astonished at the vehicle sent to invite them to dinner with the governor and his family. When the viceroy later gave them the wheat they had asked for and granted them leave, they were surprised and scared, as if plagued by a sense of foreboding.

On the way home, they were stopped by some Egyptian soldiers who checked their sacks. A silver cup was found in Benjamin's. Joseph had instructed his men to hide it there to put his brothers to a final test. On their return to the palace, Joseph revealed his true identity and tested their love for Benjamin, saying that he would keep the boy who had stolen the cup. The brothers stepped forward and begged Joseph not to do it. They were scared of having to return a second time to their father with news that he'd lost another son. Moved by the gesture, Joseph invited them to go back to Canaan and bring their father and the rest of the family to Egypt.

Jacob was initially reluctant to leave the land of his forefathers but decided, in the end, to tackle the journey.

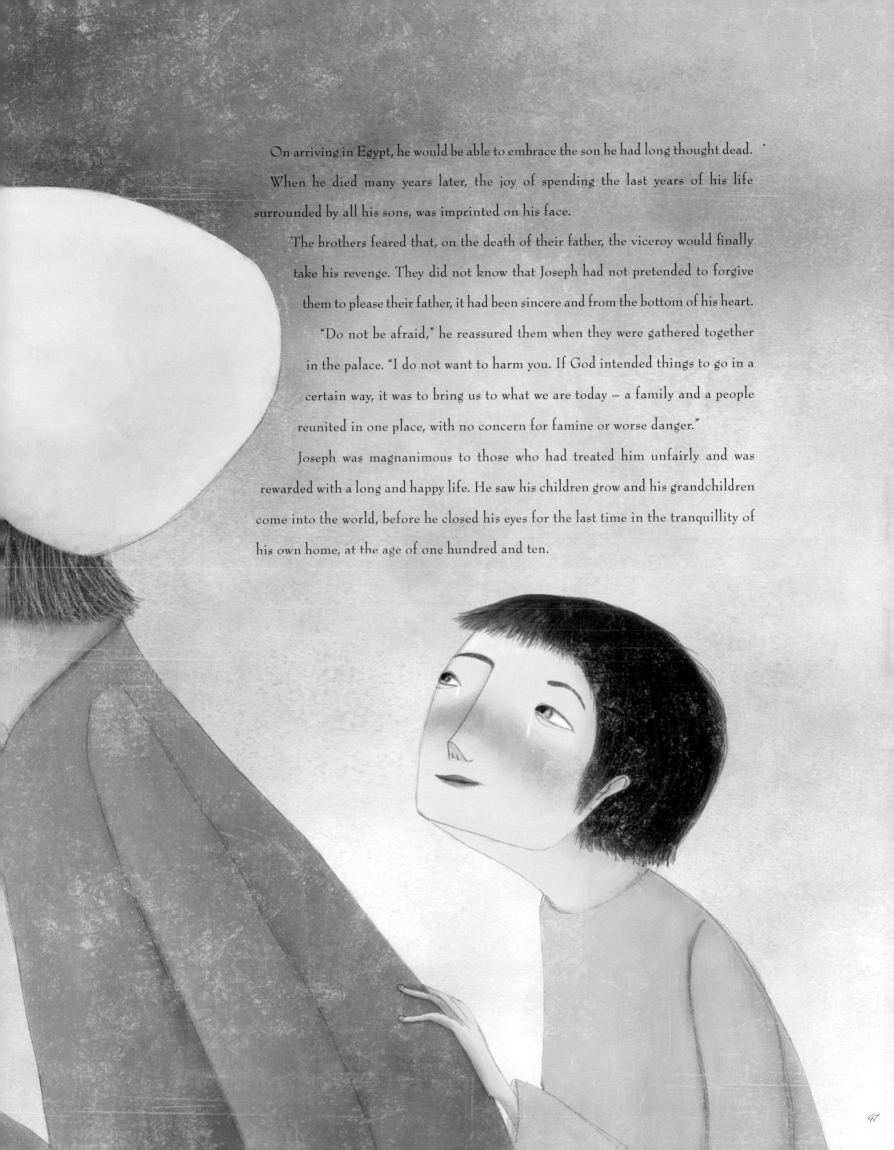

On arriving in Egypt, he would be able to embrace the son he had long thought dead.
When he died many years later, the joy of spending the last years of his life surrounded by all his sons, was imprinted on his face.

The brothers feared that, on the death of their father, the viceroy would finally take his revenge. They did not know that Joseph had not pretended to forgive them to please their father, it had been sincere and from the bottom of his heart.

"Do not be afraid," he reassured them when they were gathered together in the palace. "I do not want to harm you. If God intended things to go in a certain way, it was to bring us to what we are today — a family and a people reunited in one place, with no concern for famine or worse danger."

Joseph was magnanimous to those who had treated him unfairly and was rewarded with a long and happy life. He saw his children grow and his grandchildren come into the world, before he closed his eyes for the last time in the tranquillity of his own home, at the age of one hundred and ten.

MOSES

At the time Moses was born, Egypt was ruled by a Pharaoh who treated with great cruelty and contempt the Israelite slaves toiling in the construction of buildings, roads and tombs, or working in the fields. Despite the torment they endured, the number of slaves continued to rise and, fearing their expanding numbers could threaten the stability of his kingdom, the king ordered the sons of all slaves to be killed.

To save her son from this tragic fate, Moses' mother put the boy in a basket and left it in the tall grass along the banks of the great river Nile.

It so happened that on the same day, the Pharaoh's daughter had gone for a swim in the river, accompanied by her handmaids. On spying the basket hidden in the vegetation, she was curious and asked a servant to bring it to her. As you can imagine, she was astonished to find a crying baby in it.

Moses' older sister, who was standing nearby to watch over her brother, ran to the princess and pleaded with her to keep the baby. She also said she would find a wetnurse to feed the newborn.

The Pharaoh's daughter didn't need to be asked twice. She had fallen for the baby at first sight and had decided to bring it up as her own even before the girl had asked her.

The princess took the baby back to the palace, accompanied by the slave and the wetnurse, who was none other than the baby's real mother.

It was therefore by a strange quirk of fate, or perhaps we should say, the will of God, that Moses, son of a Hebrew slave, grew up in a Pharaoh's palace with the same honors bestowed on the rest of the royal family.

In his heart of hearts, Moses always felt different. He knew from where he had come and hated to see how the Egyptians treated his people.

Visiting his own people one day, he saw a soldier viciously beating a slave. Moses stepped in to save him but, fearing the Pharaoh might discover what he'd done, fled from the place in which he'd been born and raised, and braved the desert and the unknown.

Along the way, he stopped at a well in the village of Midian. He was thirsty and needed to regain his strength before setting off again. As he rested under a palm tree, he saw seven girls approach, leading a flock of sheep. They wanted to get water for their animals, but some shepherds stood in their way. Moses came to their rescue. The girls were so grateful to the man who had helped them that they asked their father if Moses could come to their house.

And so Moses came to live in Midian, in the house of a village priest, Jethro, where he married Zipporah, one of Jethro's daughters. None of this had happened by chance, it had been the precise will of God who had a very clear plan in mind for Moses.

He wanted to make Moses the leader of his people, to guide them to freedom and to the promised land.

Some time later, as Moses tended his father-in-law's flocks on a hillside, he witnessed a strange and unprecedented sight – a bramble bush ignited before his eyes, producing clear, bright flames.

The most disconcerting thing was that the fire did not recede as time went on, seemingly destined for burn for eternity. Moses heard a voice calling him from the flames, "Moses! Moses!"

Despite the fear he felt, Moses made to go closer, but the flames stopped him. "Come no nearer without taking off your shoes, for here you walk on holy ground. I am your God and the God of your fathers."

Moses did as the voice commanded, and also hid his face with a cloth to stop himself from seeing God or from being burned.

God spoke again, explaining to Moses the reason for their encounter. "I have seen the misery of my people in Egypt and I can no longer ignore their cries for my help and to be freed from the oppression they suffer every day under the Pharaoh's army. Of all men, I have chosen you for this important task. You must return to the land from which you fled, free all Hebrew slaves and lead them to a place in which they can live and prosper in peace."

Moses was deeply shocked at God's words. He knew his people suffered in a strange land, he had seen it with his own eyes and he knew something had to be done, but why him, why was he the one to intervene? Who would listen to him and follow him out of Egypt? How would he convince the Pharaoh to release the slaves?

"How will I..." he stammered, failing to put his doubts into words.

"You will tell my children that it is I, their God, who sends you," God answered from the burning bush. "If you do as I say, they will believe you and together you will go to the Pharaoh to ask for the freedom that is rightfully theirs. Unfortunately, the king has a hard and obstinate heart and he will not grant you permission to go, so I will make it so that you can perform wonders which will eventually convince the king."

Despite God's reassurance, Moses was doubtful. He was not convinced the people would listen to him or follow him. So God decided to show Moses his might and give him the power to perform extraordinary wonders.

"That staff in your hand," God commanded, "throw it to the ground by your feet!"

Moses obeyed and the stick turned to a snake on hitting the ground.

"Now," God continued, "pick it up by the tail."

Although he was afraid the snake might bite him, Moses obeyed God's command and picked up the snake, which turned back into a stick in his hand.

After these and many other wonders, one last doubt remained in Moses' heart. He had always believed himself a man of action, a practical person, and had no idea how he would learn to speak to the crowd or, worse still, converse with the Pharaoh.

"I am not an orator," he finally said. "How will I ever convince my people to follow me and the king to let them go?"

"You will go with your brother Aaron," God reassured him once again. "You will tell Aaron what you want to say and he, who knows what to do, will proclaim your message to the Hebrew slaves and to the king."

When God finished, the fire went out and Moses remained on the hilltop to think about what had happened. Tormented by the thought of what lay ahead but reassured by God's words, he descended the mountain and returned to the house of his father-in-law where he gathered together his meagre belongings, his wife and his children, and, taking leave of the peaceful life he'd led in Midian, set off for Egypt on the back of a donkey.

In the middle of the desert, Moses was joined by his brother Aaron, sent by God to help him. When the two men arrived back in Egypt, they told the Hebrew people of the salvation that awaited them and the people who had rushed to listen to them believed what they said.

The Pharaoh was not so open to their words. Quite the opposite, he sent them away and was even more merciless to the Hebrews, ordering that they gather their own straw to make the same number of building bricks in the same time, even though their work was now double.

The slaves remonstrated with Moses and Aaron for angering the Pharaoh and making their lives even harder than they already were.

Drawing strength from God's words, Moses reassured them and promised he would put things right with the Pharaoh and lead them to freedom.

On returning to the Pharaoh, Moses issued a stern warning. "If you do not let God's people go, a plague will fall on your kingdom."

The king was unmoved by what he heard, so Moses struck the water of the River Nile with his stick. It turned to blood, killing all the fish swimming in it and making it impossible for anyone to draw water to drink or to water their fields.

After the water turned to blood, God sent a plague of frogs. From east to west, north to south, everywhere the eye turned, frogs jumped and chased each other. Nowhere remained untouched by the hundreds of croaking frogs which had invaded buildings and land. Even the desert swarmed with thousands of the creatures.

Yet the Pharaoh's heart remained unyielding and cold. And so came swarms of gnats and flies which, like the frogs before them, invaded Egypt, stripping it of its beauty and making life difficult. In fact, it was impossible to even breathe without swallowing the insects.

After these plagues, Moses thought the Pharaoh would relent and give in to his request, but he found himself dealing with a very stubborn man, willing to sacrifice anything to avoid freeing his slaves.

Moses announced that a fifth plague would descend on Egypt. Very quickly, all cattle owned by the Egyptians inexplicably died while the animals of the Hebrews were untouched by the mortal illness.

But once again, the Pharaoh would not be moved from his decision, stating that he would never grant the Hebrew people freedom to leave his kingdom.

Moses then gathered some soot in his hands, as God bade him, and threw it into the air. Fine dust fell across the country, causing festering wounds to break out on the skin of the men and animals it touched.

The wails of the infected and the baying of dogs fallen victim to the plague were not enough to convince the Pharaoh, who again refused to succumb to the will of the Hebrew God.

The seventh plague came, hailstorms which beat down on trees and buildings, followed by the octave, swarms of locusts which devoured what little crops were left after the destruction caused by the frogs, gnats and flies.

Moses made yet another visit to the Pharaoh, to plead with him to free the slaves.

"If you don't release my people from Egypt, the hand of God shall fall yet again on this land, which has endured so much already because of the coldness of your soul," he said.

"I will never free my slaves," the king replied stubbornly.

Moments later, a dense and impenetrable fog invaded the streets of the city, falling like a dark curtain over the homes and fields of the Egyptians. People could no longer see or carry out their work, and fear about what might happen next reigned supreme. Only in the homes of the slaves did a light shine bright, the light of hope that something might change.

Since the king continued to ignore the requests of Moses and Aaron, God announced that one final plague, the tenth one, would be brought on Egypt and it would result in the people being let go. "Very shortly, the Egyptians will endure the worst punishment ever, namely the death of their firstborn sons. Only then will the Pharaoh, hearing the tortured cries of his people, allow you to go. Before this happens, tell my people to mark their doors with the blood of lambs so I will know to pass over their houses. For evermore, this day shall be known as Passover."

Moses told everyone the news he'd been given, and he made ready to leave with the others.

Darkness fell as predicted. In the silent shadows of the city, the desperate cries of those who lost their sons began to be heard. Not a single Egyptian household was spared the deadly final plague.

Deeply stricken and hit personally by the divine punishment inflicted, the Pharaoh finally granted the Hebrew slaves their freedom. In a winding caravan of people, carts and animals, they set off for the land promised to them.

The slaves had hardly left when the king seemed to change his mind and ordered his officials to find out what direction the people of Israel had gone in. Realizing the king's intentions, God told Moses to head for the Red Sea to give the appearance of being trapped between the desert and the sea, and convince the Egyptians to follow them.

Indeed, as soon as the Pharaoh learned they were encamped by the sea, he sent his army after them — six hundred chariots carrying the most ruthless warriors of the kingdom.

When the slaves saw them approach, they thought the end was near, but Moses reassured them, "Do not fear, God is with us."

As he spoke, Moses lifted up his staff to the sea and the water immediately parted before their astonished eyes. Where there had been waves, there was now a pathway of soils between walls of water. The people were scared but Moses urged them to keep going because the Pharaoh's troops were closing in.

Despite their fear about what might happen, the liberated slaves advanced as Moses bid them. When the last of the group finally reached the other side, the water flowed back and covered the pathway, sweeping the king's soldiers and their chariots under the waves. The people of Israel were finally free from Egyptian oppression.

As they struggled on, in a long line in the hot sun, they sang a song of victory.

"I will sing unto the Lord, for he hath triumphed gloriously; the Lord is my strength and my song."

They didn't know, nor was Moses aware, that it would take them many years to reach the land that God had chosen for them.

Some months later, in the Sinai desert, Moses climbed to the mountaintop and, as had happened with the burning bush, God appeared to him. He had come to announce a list of laws that Moses and the Israelite community would have to follow religiously. As Moses transcribed the ten commandments on two tablets and listened carefully to the instructions God had in mind for his people, the Israelites who had set up camp at the foot of the mountain decided to build an image of a god that they could worship. Gold from melted jewellery and utensils was used to cast a calf that they could kneel before and give sacrifice to.

God became angry when he saw what they had done and promised merciless punishment, but Moses begged God not to inflict more suffering on his people and to forgive them. Moses' words, filled with love, convinced God and he decided not to punish the Israelites for their golden calf.

When he descended from the mountain, Moses nevertheless wanted to give the people a powerful message to make them understand the wrong they had done in creating a pretend god. Before their eyes, he destroyed both the tablets bearing the commandments and the calf, reiterating that they must worship only one god - the God in the sky. Moses then returned to ask the Lord what he should do next on his mission and God ordered him to rewrite the commandments on new tablets and give them to the people.

And so Moses led his people not only to freedom, but also to the conquest of a special, unique and loving relationship with God, who had secured them their freedom.

It took several more years of pilgrimage, hardship and unexpected events before they reached the promised land, but the way had been marked for evermore.

Moses never saw the place God had promised them. He died, on Mount Nebo, just before they crossed into it, but his soul was at peace. He had obtained everything he had ever dreamed for himself and for the people he had led.

SAMSON

All children are special, although some more than others. God chooses them for the great feats they perform and causes their birth to be seen as a miracle. This is what happened to Samson, who was born to become a hero, a savior of his people.

In these times, the Israelites were subjugated to the Philistines, who treated them with scorn and prevented them from living as they would have liked. Many people hoped someone might come along and help them regain their freedom.

In one of the cities administered by the Philistines there lived Manoah, a kind and reverent Israelite, married to an equally good and religious woman. Unfortunately, and to their great sorrow, the couple were childless. An angel visited the woman one day and announced she would soon be a mother. The woman was surprised, even more so when she learned that the child, to be consecrated to God from conception, would live his life by some very specific rules. He would never eat impure foods, for example, or cut his hair.

Fearing she may not have fully understood the words of the divine messenger, the woman called her husband, to whom the angel repeated the precepts by which they would be required to abide.

It was under such auspices that Samson was born. As he grew, his strength and courage were so great he became famous, and the young boy was feared and respected wherever he went. But in tandem with these qualities, Samson had a predisposition that caused him not to see the dangers that lay on his path and to get into trouble.

Indeed, in Timnah he fell hopelessly in love with a young Philistine girl and determined to marry her, despite the disapproval of his parents who feared serious disaccord between their son and his wife's family.

Their fears were justified. Incomprehension between Samson and the Philistines led to armed conflict, after which the young man was taken prisoner by the people of Judah, who feared reprisals by the Philistines. As Samson was being led to the latter, he managed to free himself. The tight bindings were unable to contain the might of his muscles, and they snapped, crumpling to his feet like charred flax. Free to fight back once again, he grabbed the closest thing to hand, the jawbone of a dead donkey and swung it like an iron mace, quickly striking down an army of one thousand men.

On conclusion of this great feat, Samson called to God for some water and, miraculously, a fountain gurgled forth at his feet.

Following these events, Samson moved to Gaza, and thus to the Valley of Sorek, where he met a beautiful woman with whom he became infatuated. Her name was Delilah but her beauty hid a secret — she had been instructed by Philistine princes to find out everything she could about their enemy.

And so it was that with great artifice and cunning Delilah tried to discover Samson's secret. If she could find out, the Philistines would be able to defeat him once and for all.

For a long time, Samson lied to Delilah, telling her he could be beaten if he were to be bound with seven fresh bowstrings, or with new ropes, or if the braids on his head were secured to a door. Each time the woman told the Philistines, who tried, unsuccessfully, to do what had been suggested.

A day came, however, when Samson was no longer able to deceive Delilah —
he loved her too much to continue in his deceit.

"You must know," he said, "that my strength lies in my hair, which has never
been cut. If someone were to cut it, I would be as weak as any other man."

When night came, Delilah put Samson to sleep on her lap and cut his hair.

The Philistines, who had been waiting outside, burst into the room, blinded
Samson and took him to Gaza where he was put in shackles and made to turn
the grindstone.

Humiliated and scorned, Samson spent his days in the depths of despair,
while all the time his hair began to grow again.

The Philistine rulers decided to offer a sacrifice to their god Dagon. Hundreds
of people had gathered in the great ceremonial room and Samson was led in to
entertain them as court jester.

Samson used the opportunity to execute God's plan. Resting against the
pillars on which the temple stood, he cried, "Lord, I beg you, restore the strength
I was given at birth. Let me die with the Philistines!" Then he broke the pillars
holding up the temple and brought the building down on them. And so Samson
met his fate, a hero who had lost his way on account of a deceitful love, but
ultimately recovered his lost vigor and courage to let fate take its course.

DAVID AND GOLIATH

Imagine a young child, a little bigger than you, taking on a giant. Sounds incredible, doesn't it? Yet, it's what David, the boy who became king of Israel, did. But first things first…

At the time of this story, Israel's army was camped at Ephes Dammim, ready to go to battle against the army of the Philistines, gathered nearby and poised for the imminent clash.

The Philistine's champion, a certain Goliath from Gath, a seemingly invincible man of immense proportions and winner of countless battles, would emerge from his tent every day - clad in heavy armor that gleamed in the sun and brandishing weapons like mere twigs in his hands - and dare soldiers of the enemy army to face him in a duel.

The Israelites were scared by the mere roar of Goliath's booming voice and refused to fight a warrior of his stature. This had led to a stalemate and no one knew how to resolve it.

David, a young, red-haired boy who normally helped with his father's flocks, came to the camp one day. He'd only come to check how his brothers were getting on and take their pay back to his father, but he was fascinated by Goliath and became curious about the nature of the problem.

Saul, the king of Israel, learned of the boy's presence and his curiosity, and summoned him to demand an explanation.

Without waiting for the king to address him, David said, "I will fight for you!" Surprised, Saul replied, "But you are just a boy, what makes you think you can take on a strong and able warrior?"

David reassured him, "I have faced beasts of all kinds, like lions and bears, taking my father's sheep to pasture, and I have always overcome them because I have God on my side."

Saul tried to convince the boy to at least don some
armor, but David preferred to brave the enemy with only
his trusted sling and five stones gathered from a brook.

When Goliath saw him approach, he burst out
laughing then, serious once again, threatened to smash
him to pieces and feed his body to the animals.

David replied that, with God's help, he would
beat the giant, whose death would bring about the
fall of the entire Philistine army. David advanced
fearlessly toward the great warrior, withdrew a stone
from his pouch, placed it in the sling, and fired it at
his opponent's forehead. Goliath fell to the ground.
David went straight over to the giant and cut off his head
with his own sword.

The Philistines fled the instant they saw what had
happened, the Israelite soldiers close behind them.

David was hailed in triumph and praised for his deeds.
A young boy had beaten a warrior with guile and, most
importantly, through his faith in God. All he had needed was
a sling and immense courage to get the better of a warrior
who believed in nothing other than his own strength.

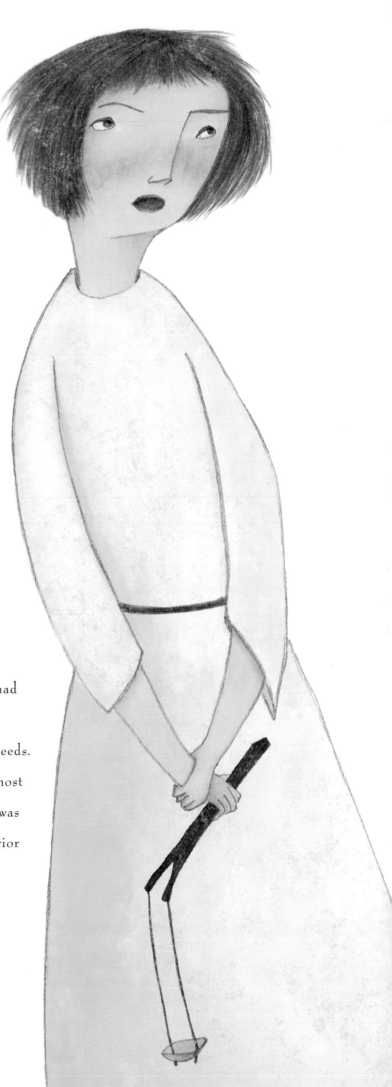

SOLOMON

Heroes are usually characterized by their bravery and strength, on rare occasions they are also endowed with great wisdom, a gift that God grants to very few. Solomon was one of the fortunate champions of antiquity who was given the chance to be wiser than any other man on Earth. It was Solomon himself, responding to God one day, who asked for such a gift. As king, he could have asked for riches, eternal life, beauty, strength, everything a powerful man might desire, but instead, he had begged the Lord to be forever guided by reason, that he might be a good leader of the kingdom left to him by his father David.

His great wisdom became the topic of much rumor and people travelled from far and wide to his palace to put his good judgment to the test.

Two women came to stand before him one day, both claiming to be the real mother of the same child.

"This woman and I," the first woman began, "lived in the same house when we both gave birth to a baby. I fell asleep with my baby beside me one night, but when I awoke the morning after, my baby was dead. When I looked more closely, I saw the dead baby wasn't the son I had borne but the other woman's, who had stolen mine when her own baby died."

"That's not true!" the other woman protested when it was her turn to speak. "The child in my arms is the one I bore and kept with me from that moment. This woman lost her baby and wants to replace him with mine, but I will never allow it!"

Having heard both versions, Solomon thought for a while then left the room. He returned seconds later holding a long, sharp sword in his hand.

"Since we cannot know who the child really belongs to and you both want him, I will now cut the child in half so you can each have a part," Solomon ruled imperiously, leaving the people in the room speechless.

"No, don't do it!" one of the two women screamed, agonized. "I'd rather my son lived with her than die."

"Do it!" the other woman cried in response, "Then we will both be happy."

Solomon smiled, now he knew which of the two women was the true mother of the child.

"Only a mother would do anything for her child, renouncing the chance to raise him to keep him from harm. The woman willing to kill the child is lying and does not deserve any pity. Give the baby to the first woman."

This was only one of Solomon's many judgments and fame of his wisdom spread far and wide, even travelling beyond his kingdom and into distant lands.

News had also reached the Queen of Sheba, who was so fascinated by the idea of the wise Solomon that she decided to make the long journey to test his knowledge. On reaching the king's court, she began to question him, devising a series of intricate stratagems to try to catch him out and prove he was a man like any other. In the end, she had to admit that Solomon possessed something divine, something out of the ordinary, and she complimented him on his wit and intelligence.

When the Queen was led through the rooms of the palace to witness their splendor, she was doubly surprised – despite being accustomed to ostentation and wealth, she could never have imagined a human mind able of conceiving something so grand and perfect as that wonderful palace.

Before taking her leave of Solomon, she decided to give him a tangible sign of her appreciation. She brought him one hundred and twenty gifts of gold and large quantities of aromatic spices and priceless stones.

Solomon accepted the gifts out of respect for his guest, but it was the queen's words he most appreciated – "Blessed be your kingdom, the people who surround you, the country that benefits from your leadership and God, who gave you such wisdom."

Indeed, being wiser than any man, Solomon knew that "a good name is worth more than great wealth, respect more than gold and silver."

JONAH

Events involving the prophet Jonah were extraordinary and miraculous, the most incredible to ever happen to a man — a turbulent trip at sea, a close encounter with a creature of monstrous proportions and preaching in a foreign land.

Why did they all happen? Because God wanted to test Jonah who, in his heart of hearts, doubted the message he had received.

The Lord appeared to Jonah one day and asked him to go to the city of Nineveh to convert the people who had become wicked and dishonest.

But Jonah was afraid, believing the task too difficult to complete. Instead, he went in the opposite direction and boarded a ship bound for Tarshish.

The ship had just left port when a terrible storm broke. The waves were big enough to capsize the craft and winds so powerful they ripped the sails, stopping them from sailing in the right direction.

The sailors were frightened and wondered what would happen to them, now that they were at the mercy of the waves and the storm which raged around them. Jonah, who knew only too well that the storm had been sent by God because he had not kept his promise, took pity on the terrified men and told them that, to placate God's fury, they should throw him into the sea and leave him to his fate.

Reluctantly, the crew did as they were instructed, and Jonah found himself in the water, which had all of a sudden become flat.

There were more trials in store for Jonah. God sent a large fish to devour him. For three days and three nights, Jonah was held captive in the monster's stomach but after humbly begging the Lord's forgiveness, was freed on the seashore.

"Will you now go to Nineveh as I asked?" God asked Jonah again.

Without answering, Jonah set off for the city of sin, wishing to please the Lord. On his arrival, he began to preach the word of the Lord and very quickly rid the people of the wickedness that had taken over their souls.

Instead of rejoicing at his success, Jonah was furious. Deep down, he'd wanted the people of Nineveh to be indifferent to his message and for God to raze the city to the ground.

To prove to Jonah he was mistaken, God caused a leafy castor oil plant to grow over the hut Jonah had built just outside the city walls. The prophet was very happy because the plant provided shade he could sleep more easily under. But the next day, a worm chewed the plant's roots and the plant withered.

Lying in his house, hot in the scorching rays of the sun, Jonah wished to die.

But God said, "You are angry with a castor oil plant you did not tend and which grew and withered in only a short time, yet I should not be concerned with the fate of an entire city that is home to thousands of people?"

Jonah understood. The Lord's mercy was too big for a prophet to comprehend. Nineveh may have done wrong, but the repentance the people had shown fully justified their salvation.

DANIEL IN THE LION'S DEN

During the reign of King Darius the Mede in Persia, there lived a righteous and reverent man, a loyal servant of his king and strict observer of the Law of God. His name was Daniel and it was to Daniel that the king assigned an important role in government, making him his equal in the most important decisions. This appointment caused a stir in the royal palace, arousing intense jealousy in the hearts of the other officials assigned more minor responsibilities. They schemed together to find something of which to accuse poor Daniel, who was oblivious to what was being plotted behind his back.

Unable to find anything in his behavior that could cast Daniel in a poor light, the officials decided to set a trap. They requested a private audience with the king and asked him to reconfirm an ancient law whereby anyone praying for more than thirty days to a god or a man that was not the king would be put to death. On seeing Darius' perplexity over whether to sign the decree, they pointed out that it was essential to restore the glorious past of the Medes and Persians.

The king finally accepted to sign the injunction, not realizing his commissioners intended it as a way of condemning Daniel who, in line with his precepts, opened his window towards Jerusalem and the Holy Land three times a day to pray to the Lord God.

Daniel knew about the law but decided not to stop praying because he was sure he was doing nothing wrong; if anything, he was doing what the Lord God wished of him. He wasn't to know the commissioners were secretly spying on him in order to refer his guilt back to the king.

After the prescribed time, the commissioners rushed straight to Darius to accuse Daniel. For a whole day, the king refused to order Daniel's capture, he was fond of the man and knew he had done nothing wrong. However, forced by a law that allowed no revocation, he had to capitulate. Daniel was arrested and left in the lion's den to be torn apart by the beasts. A heavy stone was set over the pit to stop him from escaping, and the king made if official by placing his own seal on top.

Darius spent the night fasting, lying awake and thinking about the fate of his most loyal servant. When the sun rose, he dressed and rushed to the lion's pit in the hope a miracle might have occurred and Daniel was still alive.

"Daniel, please, talk to me! Tell me that your God has saved you from the lions!" he shouted.

"Oh my King," Daniel replied from the pit, "It happened just as you described. My God sent an angel to shut the lions' mouths. He didn't want me to die because he looked into my heart and found no sin, not against him or against you."

Darius cried tears of joy and ordered Daniel to be pulled from the lion's den. The commissioners who had behaved so despicably, condemning an innocent man, were to be put there in his place.

For the rest of his days, Daniel was respected and esteemed by his king and the people of Persia – he was the man whose immense faith had saved him from the lions.

MANUELA ADREANI, was born in Rome and later moved to Turin where she currently lives. After completing a diploma in illustration, she worked as a graphic designer before moving into the world of animation.

She won a scholarship for a masters in animation at IED Turin then worked for the Lastrego and Testo studio on the television series *The Adventures of Aladdin* and *Amita in the Jungle*, produced and broadcast by RAI, and on the short film *Creation*, made for the eponymous book by Carlo Fruttero.

In 2011, she ventured into freelance illustration, working with Benchmark and Scholastic India.

Manuela was among the winners of the illustration competition held to commemorate the 130th anniversary of the publication of Pinocchio.

In recent years, she has illustrated several titles for White Star Kids.

Graphic Layout
PAOLA PIACCO

WSkids
WHITE STAR KIDS

White Star Kids® is a registered trademark property of White Star s.r.l.

© 2018, 2019 White Star s.r.l.
Piazzale Luigi Cadorna, 6 - 20123 Milan, Italy
www.whitestar.it

Revised Edition

Translation: Denise Muir

ISBN 978-88-544-1353-5
1 2 3 4 5 6   23 22 21 20 19

Printed in China